The Moon is a Woman

AF669463

Natalie Rivera

BookLeaf Publishing

Presentation by *BookLeaf Publishing*

Web: www.bookleafpub.com

E-mail: info@bookleafpub.com

ISBN: 9789357617017

First edition 2022

To my children, Bianca and Xavier, whose love has always been the guiding light of the full moon on our darkest nights.

ACKNOWLEDGEMENT

The list of those I am grateful for could wrap around this world an infinite number of times. Firstly, I must acknowledge my mother and sister for their constant support and guidance. I would be nothing without them. Secondly, I want to thank my partner, whose love has unlocked so many doors I thought were forever closed. And lastly, thank you to my teachers throughout life, whether in school or simply those who have given me the gift of some insight they had.

PREFACE

A collection of poems following the phases of the ever waxing and waning journey through womanhood. Follow a woman's journey from childhood to motherhood. From first loves, to divorce, to loving herself. The voice changes, but the heart of who she is becomes bolder and stronger with time.

Come in, Come in, Sweet Dreamer - Age 7

Come in, come in, Sweet Dreamer.
Come sit by my fireside.
We can laugh and talk,
but one thing we must do is tell stories of Fairies and Gnomes,
so that we may see the moon.

Come in, Come in, Sweet Dreamer,
so, we can see the moon.

Don't make me remind you!

Just Natalie - Age 12

Sometimes I look,
I see with my eyes,
the world is marble with people inside.
We're all running 'round,
like the sky's falling down.
But it's not, so stop,
and breathe.

Sadness will fall,
and happiness too.
'Cause there are those days,
he'll look down to you,
and say,
Just Natalie, Just Natalie
Tonight.

Rain is falling on her hair.
Her smile is as wide,
as the sky that breathes the morning air.
And you wonder why the world goes 'round.
It's Just Natalie,
Just Natalie,
tonight.

He told her so,

that he tries so hard,
to let the people, know his thoughts inside.
And they do, they always do.
Just Natalie, Just Natalie
Tonight.

You Can't Fight the Wind - Age 15

You can't fight the wind
because it's there,
and then it's gone.
It's delicate hands
beat you down so hard.

You can't fight the wind
because it's begging you to fly,
and the only thing that's stopping you
is the gravity and the urge to never try.

Invisible and thrilling
when it's beating at your face.
Just one more punch to throw
and then you'll call it a day.

It's said if you let it flow,
then you'll go in the right direction.

So, don't fight the wind.
Because you can't find the wind.
When wings were made to fly.

Butterfly Affect - Age 16

Innocent, with the flap of a butterfly's wings.
Big, blue eyes staring back at me.
Everything seems in slow motion,
the potion is kicking in.

Taken, with the sound of a siren,
you lose everything.
Like the bubble just burst
and the worst is yet to come.

I throw out my arms,
and spin around the room.
I can't feel and that's how I feel with you.

I am innocent with the popping of a balloon,
taken, and fly away with you.

Wildflower- Age 17

Tame that girl.
Brush her hair.
She puts on a smile,
but she's never really there.

Her mind is in the wild.
With her heart howling at the moon.
Her eyes open like wildflowers,
soaking up the sun to bloom.

You can keep her here.
Lock her up in a world that isn't real.
Fixed on the illusion of a golden-plated dream.

It never was the truth,
just a dandelion's promise.
And then the wind,
blows.

Picasso - Age 18

Two lips and four mouths,
Four noses, two mouths,
Wine like the shutters of your mind.
Not dumb, just drunk.

Sometimes when I'm running for the bathroom,
running for the phone,
running.
I think about puking.
Maybe it's from the alcohol poisoning,
or from the air I can't breathe
in an igloo made of stone.

Three years sobriety,
but what is sober?
I hate them,
I hate them all.

The ignorance.

Life is a game of hide and seek.
To find someone who will hide with you until
the end.
Maybe the world ended in your seclusion.
Neither of you know.

Is that sobriety?

Two lips, four mouths, three noses,
She falls up the stairs.

A Georgia Boy Laments - Age 19

The night wails.
Sonar of the city.
Streets move, masses of grey.
While you,
falling through,
struggle for air.

I wait behind.
Hoping one day trees and chivalry will lead you home.

I was told Magnolias die in cold,
but your roots run deep,
and somehow you find warmth
in a city of slate and stone.

Black Out - Age 20-27

The years were long, but the nights were fast.
They say no one sleeps in New York.
It's because time does not exist there.

The daily pace,
always racing,
to a finish line that didn't exist.

It was magnificent,
living like a comet.
Eventually the comet lands and the spark goes out.
It's just a giant rock remaining.

Where were you when it was time
to open your eyes,
and awake from the
black-out?

Vagabond of the Upper East Side - Age 28

Vagabond of the Upper East Side.
Miles high, but he can't fly.
The trash is where he lives,
and the gutter's not too far.
You can pay him cigarette,
or a tab at the bar.

He used to have a wife and two kids,
or so they say.
But he'd rather snort the powder,
or drink the whiskey any day.
And they pray that he'll find Jesus,
or refuge in some love.
But the chances are like a crap shoot,
and the dice are down the hole.

Hallelujah!
Hallelujah!
It's that Jeff Buckley song she liked.
He promised to be a better man,
and try to change his life.

It wasn't that he didn't love them.
It wasn't that he hadn't tried.

It was that he had to learn,
you can't run from what's inside.

Goodbye, New York - Age 29

I will miss New York.
The way humanity ebbs and flows in her waves,
and right when you're about to get off,
you get the best surge of your life.

Loving New York is like loving the most distant lover
that somehow makes you orgasm like you're soulmates.
It's like taking a walk on shrooms,
and everything is vibrant and foreign,
yet familiar all at once.

I love you New York!
You're like a whore.
We pay to be inside of you,
but the kiss is extra charge.

You're the muse, never the wife.
You're the song, never the singer.
You're the brush, never the art.
But one thing I know,
is for me,
you've been mine.

Your smile was a rainbow over the Empire State Building
the first time I wanted to leave you.
Your hug was that first Spring day
when you can feel the ice dripping from your bones.

I bid you adieu with a love in my heart.
Goodbye, Ruby Tuesday,
no one could hang a name on you.
For you, New York,
you change with every new day,
and for this, I will miss you.

Twister - Age 30

The tornado sirens were wailing.
And my dreams were so vivid.
I woke up raw.
Like someone had taken a cheese grater to my soul.
Missing you.
Just wanting your smell and the way it feels inside your arms.

Perhaps I don't miss you,
Maybe it's the nostalgia of youth.
When the sands of time felt like a Percocet induced nap on the beach,
Instead of sandpaper ripping through the pocks on the walls of the home we'd built.

Either way, my eyes stay leaking on days like this.
Puddles forming around me like an Alice in Wonderland scene.
Which reminds me of the time we tripped,
and it felt like the world was whole,
because I always felt whole with you.

Until I was completely emptied.

Cuddle Island - Age 30

And we're awake late again.
Us three.
They drove me nuts all day.
But somehow these moments seem precious.
The late-night moments.

He holds a train.
She sings.
They meet eyes and hug,
and maybe this,
this is the family I deeply needed.
Maybe as I play them feminist poems,
I'm the mom I always wanted to be.

And we're awake,
and we're holding each other.
I'm in a kimono.
They're in pull-ups and mops of curls.

Nothing can penetrate our little world.

We can travel the globe,
but all we'd ever need is in this bed.
Oceans of blankets,
mountains of pillows,

surrounding us,
in our island of cuddles.

When I hold them, I hold the world.
My whole, little world.

Fantastical Beasts - Age 30

I watch your silhouette against the white wall
and blinking green lights
of a million, mindless,
technological things.
None as fantastical as you.

The curve of your nose,
down to the most, perfect, pouty, lips.
We are made of stardust,
but no star or galaxy
is as majestic or awe-inspiring,
as you.

For in you lies the dreams of ancestors centuries past,
and for Millenia to come.
In you is hope,
much like a seed setting to spring forth
and bud into the most, fruitful flower.

I never knew I needed you,
but your very existence
has made mine of value.

The simplicity of steps,

breaths,
words,
and wishes
equals more than a million pounds of gold.

Forever I lie in astonishment
of the billions of cells
that created you,
out of me.

Once a tiny heart in an empty space,
now running through the leaves in the yard.
Crunching.
Screaming.
Laughing.

So much life.

So alive.

So happy you are mine.

All is Not Fair in Love & War - Age 31

Your smell clung to my skin
and I wore it with pride,
Although it was the opposite of honor.

I'd fallen like a soldier in the battlefield
that was our love.
You always riding away gallantly,
while my city burned down around me.

As I huffed the lingering fumes of you,
and smiled wide.
I knew the war was not over,
yet.

Situations & Ships - Age 31

As the cars fly by it sounds like waves,
(Or so you said one time as you cradled me in
the after-sex glow of situational love.)
The waves of I-75.
Ebbs and flows
Of a city alone.
Me trying to find my peace
When chaos is all, I know.

We are made of water,
And moondust,
And stardust,
And all the things that let us go.

We hold on tighter
And pretend it's love.
(But it's like holding butter,
eventually it'll melt through your hands.
Only oil and fat remain.
Like the shadow spots of humans after nuclear
fall-out.)

It's only as we get older and start creating our
own peace
that we realize,

Sometimes the place that feels like home isn't
happy.
It's just familiar.
(Like the way ice clinking against a glass
sounded like your father coming home.)

As the cars fly by, it sounds like waves.
This time, you are not by my side.
I have grown tired of waiting for validation in
the tides of your love.
The ever-changing cycles of the moon and your
affection
could not hold me anymore.

But I still like to think,
maybe,
you're in one of those cars,
swishing by,
regretfully knowing you
could've drowned in my love,
yet, you chose to keep searching for shore.

Sponge - Age 32

"These are the years."
They say.
Soak it all up.

And I'm trying to have a heart so vast
that it could suck up the Atlantic Ocean.
I'm trying to remember every smile,
Every year,
Every tiny detail.
The smell of their baby breath,
The sound of the crunching leaves under their toddler toes,
but there are times I drown under the weight of it all.
Days I fail to surf the wave,
and instead tumble into the dark depths of my insecurities.
I hope they remember the days we played in the waves in the sun,
far more than they remember the overcast days of solace.
I hope they remember the sandcastles we built,
every time there's turbulence in our home.
For this is all ephemeral,
but I need them to know what we have

is built on a foundation of stone.

"These are the years."
They say.
Soak it all up.
But I’ve watched enough people drown to know
it’s a fine line between, absorption and
consumption.
I just want to be able to take it all in,
without it taking me
UNDER.

Cup Runneth Over - Age 32

Double petaled lily,
like some good luck omen from above.
My hibiscus all are blooming,
a lot of hard work, a lot of love.

I prayed for all this honey, all this nectar of the gods.
And now it's here,
I'm overwhelmed.
It's truly just too much.

We are all forever wanting,
all the things, all the love.
But the truth about abundance,
is it's not always about how much.

For a river overflowing, is a curse upon the land.
And too much rain will drown you, if you don't know how to swim.

Real bounty comes from careful planning.
Just planting seeds won't make them grow.
It's the tender, caring, farmer's hands that spring forth life from below.

We are all just plants called people.
Needing water, sun and care.
It's not an easy journey,
You must tend your inner garden,
to see your fruits come to bear.

Double petaled lily,
like some good luck omen from above,
My heart is now blooming,
a lot of hard work, a lot of love.

Thoughts on Loss- Age 33

I bled for 30 days straight.
I didn't die, but I felt like death.
And something that wasn't alive yet,
didn't get to be born.

My own skin smelled like a different person.
They say a mother takes on each child's DNA,
and since mine didn't get to fully form,
Now I lived with the DNA of a bloody mass.
Would that forever change my DNA too?

In a year of so much loss,
it felt almost trivial to mourn a mass of cells.
But maybe I was finally crying over all of it.
The friend that would never see her kids grow
up,
The world imploding with each passing day.
Maybe I wasn't just miscarrying an embryo,
maybe I was miscarrying some lingering hope
that things were okay.

And for a little time,
I had two hearts in me.
And in a world that I could hardly carry with
one heart,
I suppose the second one had to give itself up.

Survivor's Remorse - Age 33

We always said if there was nuclear fall-out,
we'd swim towards the city together.
Because being linked together in disaster was
our natural state.

When the bottom finally fell out,
I was nowhere near the fatal storm.
And for that I couldn't help but feel at fault.
Like I failed you by not drowning in the same
river of self-hate and fear.
Because of that,
I spent months trying to piece it together,
and be the most helpful,
the most yours.
Because by the end helping you,
(Fixing the brakes on a car going nowhere fast.)
was all I knew how to do.

Loving you was chaos.
Like living in a tornado.
But I grew up in the Deep South,
so the heavy air and green skies always felt like
home.
Then one day I realized,
I could have sunny days and daisies,
and I left that all behind.

(The life made of swirling skies that would one
day take you away,
with the sweep of a funnel cloud.)

This is where you get off,
but my train goes on.
And there are dark tunnels ahead,
that I wish you were there to hold my hand
through.
I wish we could defeat one more mugger
together.
But, time doesn't heal all things.
(Ask the carpet in my car that reeks of yeast
from the time that we broke wine, while loading
groceries,
that one fall day.)

You're gone,
but I'm reminded daily
of the beautiful times we had.
The adventures.
It all feels so trivial now.

I will no longer swim towards fall-out.
I'm too busy building towers to the sky.
And when I get there,
I hope,
just maybe,
You will be there to greet me at the door.

A lot to unpack here... - Age 33

You will feel lonely,
if only for a little while,
but perhaps it may be a long while.
The shadow of that loneliness will one day pass.

You will fight the darkest places of your mind.
You might even find the most perfect, beautiful love,
And it may leave,
but, the one who can hold your heart like a kitten
whilst removing its fleas
(firmly, yet tenderly.)
That will be the one that teaches you,
that some people stay.

You may feel sick with aches and fever.
You may shiver in the darkness of your room.
But, you will feel the way your heart grows like the grinch,
as the family you'd hoped for and planned for
begins to develop in front of your eyes.
(Like a roll of 35mm film that's been waiting in an old suitcase for you to discover.)

And when you realize that you've finally
stopped hopping on the next train to heartbreak,
you will have a lot to unpack.
And I hope you'll hang the clothes long enough
to watch the wrinkles disappear.

The Moon is A Woman - Age 33

The moon is a woman,
elusive and unsure.
She'll give you just enough,
to keep you wanting more.

The moon is a woman.
That's why man has always
tried to conquer her.
Just because you've touched her surface,
doesn't make her yours.

Waxing and waning.
Creation and destruction.
A constant state of evolution.
Wait for tomorrow,
a different woman will be outside your door.

The moon is a woman.
Vibrant and glowing.
She's found peace in the craters of her heart,
and embraced the voluptuous abundance found
in her curves.

There were nights when she hid in the shadows
of herself.
There were days where she stood beside the sun.
Constant and steadfast,
in her wavering way.

The hourglass keeps running.
The tides keep changing.
The moon is a woman.
She will come and go.
She will disappear and grow.

Just enjoy this phase.

www.ingramcontent.com/pod-product-compliance
Lightning Source LLC
Chambersburg PA
CBHW062204160726
48282CB00027B/985
9789357617017